BRIAN PATTEN is one of Britai[...]
ing the success of the ground-[...]
The Mersey Sound (with Roger McGough and the late Adrian
Henri), he has gone on to develop a career as both poet and
children's author. His collections for adults include *Armada*,
Storm Damage and *Grinning Jack*, while his collections for
children include the bestselling *Gargling with Jelly*, *Thawing
Frozen Frogs* and *The Story Giant*, published by Harper-
Collins. Brian Patten's work has been widely translated. He is
a Fellow of the Royal Society of Literature and in 2001 was
honoured with the Freedom of the City of Liverpool.

Visit www.AuthorTracker.co.uk for exclusive information
on your favourite HarperCollins authors.

BRIAN PATTEN

Collected Love Poems

From the Library of
Dr Chris Waller

HARPER PERENNIAL
London, New York, Toronto and Sydney

Harper Perennial
An imprint of HarperCollins*Publishers*
77–85 Fulham Palace Road
Hammersmith
London w6 8jb

www.harperperennial.co.uk

This edition published by Harper Perennial 2007

2

Copyright © Brian Patten 1992, 1995, 1996, 2007

Some of these poems have previously been published in the following
collections of Brian Patten's poetry: *Love Poems* (Flamingo, 1992);
Grinning Jack (Flamingo, 1995); *Storm Damage* (Flamingo, 1995); and
Armada (Flamingo, 1996).

Brian Patten asserts the moral right to
be identified as the author of this work

A catalogue record for this book is available from the British Library

ISBN-13 978-0-00-724649-6
ISBN-10 0-00-724649-8

Set in Linotype Minion by
Rowland Phototypesetting Ltd, Bury St Edmunds, Suffolk

Printed and bound in Great Britain by Clays Ltd, St Ives plc

CONTENTS

Not Only

Not only the leaf shivering with delight
No,
Not only the grass shrugging off the weight of frost
No,
Not only the taste of your skin
No,
Not only steam rising from the morning river
No,
Not only the heart on fire
No,
Not only the sound of the sunflower roaring
No,
Not only love's resurrection
No,
Not only the cathedral window deep in the raindrop
No,
Not only the sky as blue and smooth as an egg
No,
Not only the fairytale of forever
No,
Not only the wings of the crane fly consumed by fire
No,
Not only these things
No,
But without you none of these things

Into My Mirror Has Walked

Into my mirror has walked
A woman who will not talk
Of love or of its subsidiaries,
But who stands there,
Pleased by her own silence.
The weather has worn into her
All seasons known to me.
In one breast she holds
Evidence of forests,
In the other, of seas.

I will ask her nothing yet
Would ask so much
If she gave a sign –

Her shape is common enough,
Enough shape to love.
But what keeps me here
Is what glows beyond her.

I think at times
A boy's body
Would be as easy
To read light into,
I think sometimes
My own might do.

These Songs Were Begun
One Winter

These songs were begun one winter
When on a window thick with frost
Her finger drew
A map of all possible directions,
When her body was one possibility among
Arbitrary encounters
And loneliness sufficient to warrant
A meeting of opposites.

How easily forgotten then
What was first felt –
An anchor lifted from the blood,
Sensations intense as any lunatic's,
Ruined by unaccustomary events,
Let drop because of weariness.

The Ambush

When the face you swore never to forget
Can no longer be remembered,
When a list of regrets is torn up and thrown away
Then the hurt fades,
And you think you've grown strong.
You sit in bars and boast to yourself,
'Never again will I be vulnerable.
It was an aberration to be so open,
A folly, never to be repeated.'
How absurd and fragile such promises.
Hidden from you, crouched
Among the longings you have suppressed
And the desires you imagine tamed,
A sweet pain waits in ambush.
And there will come a day when in a field
Heaven's mouth gapes open,
And on a web the shadow
Of a marigold will smoulder.
Then without warning,
Without a shred of comfort,
Emotions you thought had been put aside
Will flare up within you and bleed you of reason.
The routines which comforted you,
And the habits in which you sought refuge
Will bend like sunlight under water,
And go astray.

Once again your body will become a banquet,
Falling heavenwards.
You will loll in spring's sweet avalanche
Without the burden of memory,
And once again
Monstrous love will swallow you.

A Blade of Grass

You ask for a poem.
I offer you a blade of grass.
You say it is not good enough.
You ask for a poem.

I say this blade of grass will do.
It has dressed itself in frost,
It is more immediate
Than any image of my making.

You say it is not a poem,
It is a blade of grass and grass
Is not quite good enough.
I offer you a blade of grass.

You are indignant.
You say it is too easy to offer grass.
It is absurd.
Anyone can offer a blade of grass.

You ask for a poem.
And so I write you a tragedy about
How a blade of grass
Becomes more and more difficult to offer,

And about how as you grow older
A blade of grass
Becomes more difficult to accept.

What I Need for the Present

Thanks, but please take back
the trinket box, the picture
made from butterfly wings and
the crystal glass.

Please take back the books,
the postcards, the beeswax candles,
the potted plant, the Hockney print
and the expensive pen.

Ungracious of me to say it, but
so many gifts that are given
are given in lieu of what
cannot be given.

Ungracious to say it, but
wherever I move in this room
it's not these gifts I see, but your absense
that accumulates on them like dust.

Forgive me. Your intentions
were so very kind, but here's
your box of fetters back. It's not
what I need for the present.

Through All Your
Abstract Reasoning

Coming back one evening through deserted fields
when the birds, drowsy with sleep,
have all but forgotten you,
you stop, and for one moment jerk alive.

Something has passed through you
that alters and enlightens: O
realization of what has gone and was real.
A bleak and uncoded message whispers
down all the nerves:

'You cared for her! For love you cared!'

Something has passed a finger through
all your abstract reasoning.
From love you sheltered outside of love but still
the human bit leaked in,
stunned and off-balanced you.

Unprepared, struck so suddenly by another's identity,
how can you hold on to any revelation?
You have moved too carefully through your life.
Always the light within you is hooded by
your own protecting fingers!

Song for Last Year's Wife

Alice, this is my first winter
of waking without you, of knowing
that you, dressed in familiar clothes,
are elsewhere, perhaps not even
conscious of our anniversary. Have
you noticed? The earth's still as hard,
the same empty gardens exist? It is
as if nothing special had changed.
I wake with another mouth feeding
from me, but still feel as if
love had not the right
to walk out of me. A year now. So
what? you say. I send out my spies
to find who you are living with, what
you are doing. They return, smile
and tell me your body's as firm,
you are as alive, as warm and inviting
as when they knew you first.

      Perhaps it is the winter,
its isolation from other seasons, that
sends me your ghost to witness
when I wake. Somebody came here today, asked
how you were keeping, what you were doing.
I imagine you, waking in another city,
enclosed by this same hour. So
ordinary a thing as loss comes now
and touches me.

On Time for Once

I was sitting thinking of our future
and of how friendship had overcome
so many nights bloated with pain;

I was sitting in a room that looked on to a garden
and a stillness filled me,
bitterness drifted from me.

I was as near paradise as I am likely to get again.

I was sitting thinking of the chaos
we had caused in one another
and was amazed we had survived it.

I was thinking of our future
and of what we would do together,
and where we would go and how,

when night came
burying me bit by bit,
and you entered the room

trembling and solemn-faced,
on time for once.

A Small Dragon

I've found a small dragon in the woodshed.
Think it must have come from deep inside a forest
because it's damp and green and leaves
are still reflecting in its eyes.

I fed it on many things, tried grass,
the roots of stars, hazel-nut and dandelion,
but it stared up at me as if to say, I need
food you can't provide.

It made a nest among the coal,
not unlike a bird's but larger.
It is out of place here
and is quite silent.

If you believed in it I would come
hurrying to your house to let you share my wonder,
but I want instead to see
if you yourself will pass this way.

Doubt Shall Not Make
an End of You

Doubt shall not make an end of you
Nor closing eyes lose your shape
When the retina's light fades;
What dawns inside me will light you.

In our public lives we may confine ourselves to darkness,
Our nowhere mouths explain away our dreams,
But alone we are incorruptible creatures,
Our light sunk too deep to be of any public use
We wander free and perfect without moving,

Or love on hard carpets
Where couples revolving round the room
End found at its centre –

I reach into you to reach all mankind,
And the deeper into you I reach
The deeper glows elsewhere the world
And sings of you. It says,
To love is the one common miracle.

Our love like a whale from its deepest ocean rises –

I offer this and a multitude of images,
From party rooms to oceans,
The single star and all its reflections;
Being completed we include all
And nothing wishes to escape us.

Feel nothing separate then –
We have translated each other into love
And into light go streaming.

First Love

Falling in love was like falling down the stairs
Each stair had her name on it
And he went bouncing down each one like a tongue-tied
    lunatic
One day of loving her was an ordinary year
He transformed her into what he wanted
And the scent from her
Was the best scent in the world
Fifteen he was fifteen
Each night he dreamed of her
Each day he telephoned her
Each day was unfamiliar
Scary even
And the fear of her going weighed on him like a stone
And when he could not see her for two nights running
It seemed a century had passed
And meeting her and staring at her face
He knew he would feel as he did forever
Hopelessly in love
Sick with it
And not even knowing her second name yet
It was the first time
The best time
A time that would last forever
Because it was new
Because he was ignorant it could ever end
It was endless

After Rimbaud's *Première Soirée*

Sitting half naked in my chair
she clasped her hands to her mouth
trembling with pleasure
The shadows of the cypress trees leaned into the window
to gawp at us
Her breasts were so tiny
and her hair cropped so short
she could have been a boy
but we were beyond such trifling considerations
I licked her small ankles
kissed each fragile bone
as her stomach flipped over and over
Things she had imagined so furtively and for so long
yet had dared share with no one
were coming true at last!
It is how she wanted things to be
Her feet shivered on the cool floor of the room
beating out a rhythm of pure pleasure

Now They Will Either Sleep,
Lie Still, or Dress Again

It's evening,
Over the room's silence other voices and sounds.
For them the world is a distant planet.
And lying here they are naked,
Her blonde hair falling is spread out across him.
Around her throat her mother's necklace adds
Sophistication to her clumsiness.
Let their touchings be open –
They no longer belong to a race of pale children
Whose bodies are hardly born,
Nor among the virgins hung still inside their sadness,
But waking together their world is perfect.
Littered about the room still
Are the clothes they used for meeting in.
Evening, and the sun has moved across the room.
Now they will either sleep, lie still, or dress again.

Party Piece

He said:

'Let's stay here
Now this place has emptied
And make gentle pornography with one another,
While the partygoers go out
And the dawn creeps in,
Like a stranger.

Let us not hesitate
Over what we know
Or over how cold this place has become,
But let's unclip our minds
And let tumble free
The mad, mangled crocodile of love.'

So they did,
There among the cigarettes and guinness stains,
And later he caught a bus and she a train
And all there was between them then
Was rain.

Nor the Sun Its Selling Power

They said her words were like balloons
with strings I could not hold,
that her love was something in a shop
cheap and far too quickly sold.

But the tree does not price its apples
nor the sun its selling power,
the rain does not gossip
or speak of where it goes.

When She Wakes Drenched from Her Sleep

When she wakes drenched from her sleep
She will not ask to be saluted by the light
Nor carolled by morning's squabbling birds,
Nor lying in his arms wish him repeat
The polite conversations already heard;
She'll not be loved by roses but by men,
She will glide free of sweet beauty's net
And all her senses open out
To receive each sensation for herself.
If I could be that real, that open now,
And not by half a light half lit
I would not gossip of what is beauty and what is not
Nor reduce love to a freak poem in the dark.

Dressed

Dressed you are a different creature.
Dressed you are polite, are discreet and full of friendships,
Dressed you are almost serious.
You talk of the world and of all its disasters
As if they really moved you.
Dressed you hold on to illusions.

The wardrobes are full of your disguises.
The dress to be unbuttoned only in darkness,
The dress that seems always about to fall from you,
The touch-me-not dress, the how-expensive dress,
The dress slung on without caring.
Dressed you are a different creature.

You are indignant of the eyes upon you,
The eyes that crawl over you,
That feed on the bits you've allowed
To be naked.
Dressed you are imprisoned in labels,
You are cocooned in fashions,
Dressed you are a different creature.

As easily as in the bedrooms
In the fields littered with rubble
The dresses fall from you,
In the spare room the party never reaches
The dresses fall from you.
Aided or unaided, clumsily or easily,
The dresses fall from you and then
From you falls all the cheap blossom.
Undressed you are a different creature.

The Transformation

You are no longer afraid.
You watch, still half asleep,
How dawn ignites a room;
His rough head and body curled
In awkward fashion can but please.

His face is puffed with sleep;
His body once distant from your own
Has by the dawn been changed,
And what little care you had at first
Within this one night has grown.

You smile at how those things that troubled you
Were quick to leave,
At how in their place has come a peace,
A rest once beyond imagining.

Your bodies linked, you hardly dare to move;
A new thought has now obsessed your brain:
'Come the light,
He might again have changed.'
And what you feel
You are quick to name,
And what you feel
You are quick to cage.

You watch, still half asleep,
How dawn misshapes a room;
And all your confidence by the light is drained
And still his face,
His face is still transformed.

Leavetaking

She grew careless with her mouth.
Her lips came home in the evening numbed.
Excuses festered among her words.
She said one thing, her body said another.
Her body, exhausted, spoke the truth.
She grew careless, or became without care,
Or panicked between both.

Too logical to suffer, imagining
Love short-lived and 'forever'
A lie fostered on the mass to light
Blank days with hope,
What she meant to him was soon diminished.
He too had grown careless with his mouth.
Habit wrecked them both, and wrecked
They left the fragments untouched, and left.

The Poor Fools

You ask why poets speak so often
In the language of goodbyes.
It's because beginnings take them by surprise.
Love comes and hammers them,
And then the poor fools are lost for words.
They abandon their pens, and their fingers
Itch for other things: buttons, nipples, zips –
For everything but the poor abandoned pen.

Tonight I Will Not Bother You

Tonight I will not bother you with telephones
Or voices speaking their cold and regular lines;
I'll write no more notes in crowded living rooms
Saying what and how much has changed,
But fall instead to silence and things known.

When through exhaustion you scream, throw up
Sorrow that's become a physical pain,
I'll not try and comfort you with words
That add little but darkness to ourselves
But with the body speak, its senses known.

There is no frantic hurry to love
Or press on another one's own dream.
This much I know has changed,
What was once wild is calmed,
And quieter now behind the brain
May throw more light on things;
And what starved for love survives
Whatever shadow it hunted down.

Taking what love comes makes
All that comes much easier;
Something buried deep selects what our shapes need;
The smaller habits it allows to breathe then fade,
Leaving the centre clean.

Tonight I will not bother you with excuses.
If owning separate worlds means pain
Comes more easily, and hurt
Remains a common part of us,
Then silence is best; it will allow
All doubts to strip themselves.
Then whatever's seen will surely
Be seen in its own light,
And whatever is wanted be wanted
For more than wanting's sake.

It is Time to Tidy Up Your Life

It is time to tidy up your life!
Into your body has leaked this message.
No conscious actions, no broodings
Have brought the thought upon you.
It is time to take into account
What has gone and what has replaced it.
Living your life according to no plan
The decisions were numerous and yet
The ways to go were always one.

You stand between trees this evening;
The cigarette in your cupped hand
Glows like a flower.
The drizzle falling seems
To wash away all ambition.
There are scattered through your life
Too many dreams to entirely gather.

Through the soaked leaves, the soaked grass,
The earth-scents and distant noises
This one thought is re-occurring:
It is time to take into account what has gone,
To cherish and replace it.
You learnt early enough that celebrations
Do not last forever,
So what use now the sorrows that mount up?

You must withdraw your love from that
Which would kill your love.
There is nothing flawless anywhere,
Nothing that has not the power to hurt.
As much as hate, tenderness is the weapon of one
Whose love is neither perfect nor complete.

Remembering

Not all that you want and ought not to want
Is forbidden to you,
Not all that you want and are allowed to want
Is acceptable.
Then it gets late on
And things change their value.

You are tired.
You feel the ground with your hands.
A single blade of grass appears before your eyes.
It flashes on and off,
A remnant of paradise.

And then perhaps you will remember
What you have forgotten to remember,
What should have been so easy remembering.

You will recall the hut in the morning,
And hoof-prints flooded with frost,
And how a weed and a pebble were caught once
On a cow's lip,

And perhaps how on a tremendous horse
A small boy once galloped off,
And how it was possible to do
All that now seems impossible,
All you ever wanted.

Love Lesson

When, unexpectedly, Love returns from its disappointments,
And flopping into your arms, lying says,
'This time I have come back to stay,
All other bodies were at best a compromise,'
Then if you are wise
You will choose to believe its lies.

The Innocence of Any Flesh Sleeping

Sleeping beside you I dreamt
I woke beside you;
waking beside you
I thought I was dreaming.

Have you ever slept beside an ocean?
Well yes,
it is like this.

The whole motion of landscapes, of oceans
is within her.
She is
the innocence of any flesh sleeping,
so vulnerable
no protection is needed.

In such times
the heart opens,
contains all there is,
there being no more than her.

In what country she is
I cannot tell.
But knowing –
because there is love

and it blots out all demons –
she is safe,
I can turn,
sleep well beside her.

Waking beside her I am dreaming.
Dreaming of such wakings
I am to all love's senses woken.

Someone Coming Back

Now that the summer has emptied
and laughter's warned against possessions,
and the swans have drifted from the rivers,
like one come back from a long journey
no longer certain of his country
or of its tangled past and sorrows,
I am wanting to return to you.

When love affairs can no longer be distinguished from song
and the warm petals drop without regret,
and our pasts are hung in a dream of ruins,
I am wanting to come near to you.

For now the lark's song has grown visible
and all that was dark is ever possible,
and the morning grabs me by the heart and screams,
'O taste me! Taste me please!'

And so I taste. And the tongue is nude,
the eyes awake; the clear blood hums
a tune to which the world might dance;
and love which often lived in vaguer forms
bubbles up through sorrow and laughing, screams:
'O taste me! Taste me please!'

Mindless Now

Her beauty only later becomes obvious,
rising out of her like heat,
a scent hugging him close as it can.
Caught by surprise in the flow of her
he has ceased to think of her.
He's like a grasshopper adrift on a blade of grass,
mindless now.

In Your Turning Against Walls

Sitting in a public garden, black coat
Around me, the only light that's left
Is what lingers in the grass, in lumps of soil,
In fading child voices. Here I wonder
What other lives you are involved in, how
You feel when, naked in first visited rooms
You turn, face unfamiliar walls,
Cry fake or real as someone enters.
Some lives we pass through we
Pass through blindly, echoing
Previous attachments. Arguing and then silent,
Afraid of each other but more afraid
Of what the night might not offer us,
Our boredom contents itself with hurting.
Tuned in to this century's sickness,
What we do not have is all that's wanted.
Outside how many windows does the night
Harden itself around us? Though addicted still
To love's obsessions, though
Still possible to be gentle, to drown still
In a waterfall of wind and scents,
Memory acts as a filter to any new love entering.
Sitting in a public garden, black coat around me,
No longer blind to the heart's deceptions,
I write such notes not for one singled out
But for all who, like us, are lost amongst
The day's numerous betrayals.

The Confession

When he showed her the photograph again, she said,

'Yes, I remember taking it.
I was incredibly young then.
You handed me the camera
And telling me over and over how to use it
You posed, smiling stiffly.
You were so pompous, so blind to everything.

'It was a July afternoon.
The day was hot and my body hummed.
I was bored, and in search of an adventure
That seemed beyond you.

'Yet how can I forget that day?
Look closer at the photograph.
See there in the background,
In the corner behind you,
That other boy, grinning so openly.'

She Complicates Her Life

She complicates her life.
The ghosts of what might have been
Haunt her days.
Though Love whispers, 'Stay'
She hears the opposite and turns away.
Afraid, she closes down,
And to avoid all pain
Turns back to ice again.

Perhaps

And when you turn your back something
That will not happen again happens,
And when you close your eyes perhaps
The stars rush about,
Or something changes colour.

And if you had been in a certain cafe,
In a certain street at a certain time,
Perhaps she would not have risen
And putting on a blue coat, vanished.

You hurry, and every place you pass
Pass places you have never been,
Where the future comes and goes,
Swirls round you and bypasses.

And all your dithering days you go
About the business of living,
Only for you it is not exactly living,
But filing away, ticking off, rearranging.

And nothing will ever be repeated again
Exactly as it happened,
And so much will have been missed
That has never been missed,
And yet still leaves you hungry and baffled.

The Assassination of the Morning

The morning has a hole in its side,
It rolls through the grass like a wounded bear.
Over and over it goes, clutching its wound,
Its wound fat with sorrow.

I feel nothing for the morning.
I kneel in the early grass and stare out blankly;
I stare at the blank leaves,
The leaves fat with sorrow.

Morning, the birds have come to patch you up.
They will bandage you with grass.
Morning, you are so tired.
Your eyes look terrible.

I remember how once
You were so eager to begin life,
Dressed in glittering frost you strolled
Nonchalantly down the avenues.

O Morning, it was bound to happen!

You grasp at the wet branches, the spiky thickets.
Over and over you roll, the years pouring out of you.
I wipe a razor clean of flowers, ignore the birds,
And their insistent shouting of 'Assassin'.

A Creature to Tell the Time By

I created for myself
a creature to tell the time by
– and on the lawns of her tongue
flowers grew,
sweet scented words fell
out her mouth, her eyes and paws were comforting –
and woken with her
at dawn, with living birds

humming, alien
inside my head,

I sensed inside us both
the green love that grew there yesterday
was dead.

A Suitcase Full of Dust

I packed a suitcase.
I put dust in it.
And then more dust.
I packed bits and pieces
Of what was still living.

I packed a suitcase,
A heart howled inside it.
A face stared up from it,
Its tongue wagging in the dust.

With each passing second
The complaints it made
Seemed more obsolete.
I packed a suitcase full of dust.

I went outside.
I was afraid people would stop me and ask
Why I was travelling about with dust.

There seemed nowhere to go
But to another place of dust.
I do not want dust.
My blood is slow and full of dust.
And your kiss is dust.

I do not want dust.
Your breath has changed
Pollen into dust.
I do not want dust.

Now when you speak it is simply to speak of dust.
And what was once love
Flops about in that dust.
I do not want dust.

Swearing fidelity to all
That is clean and free of dust,
I pack a suitcase full of dust.

The Mistake

Because we passed grief to and fro
toying with it,
I have shut the door of this room,

I have shut out everyone else's pain
until I can cope with my own;
tonight I'm confused enough.

For too long I have been
one of this city's strays,
yelping for attention,

part of that mass disfigured
through self-inflicted pain,
its flesh washed by exhaustion.

Because there is no pill or science
to dismiss the darkness
that is given like a gift

I have shut the door of this room;
but that too is a mistake of kinds,
for the room is in darkness,

and sinking deeper into it
the mistake becomes obvious.

In Someplace Further On

In someplace further on you seek
A sympathy that will ignite
A rose with its dying.
A dreamer by whose dreams
Love is made cankerous,
You do not accept easily
Its coming and goings.

As in all things one nature dictates
What energy is needed
To thrive, even among starlight,
So in you more intricate seasons
Plough at the blood.

Some knowledge you tried so hard
Through pain to find
One night while you slept,
Undetected, entered.

Becalmed spider, caught up within your own kill
You do not notice how the web
By a bird is shaken.

And Nothing is Ever as Perfect as You Want It to Be

You lose your love for her and then
It is her who is lost,
And then it is both who are lost,
And nothing is ever as perfect as you want it to be.

In a very ordinary world
A most extraordinary pain mingles with the small routines,
The loss seems huge and yet
Nothing can be pinned down or fully explained.

You are afraid.
If you found the perfect love
It would scald your hands,
Rip the skin from your nerves,
Cause havoc with a computed heart.

You lose your love for her and then it is her who is lost.
You tried not to hurt and yet
Everything you touched became a wound.
You tried to mend what cannot be mended,
You tried, neither foolish nor clumsy,
To rescue what cannot be rescued.

You failed,
And now she is elsewhere
And her night and your night
Are both utterly drained.

How easy it would be
If love could be brought home like a lost kitten
Or gathered in like strawberries,
How lovely it would be;
But nothing is ever as perfect as you want it to be.

Simple Lyric

When I think of her sparkling face
And of her body that rocked this way and that,
When I think of her laughter,
Her jubilance that filled me,
It's a wonder I'm not gone mad.

She is away and I cannot do what I want.
Other faces pale when I get close.
She is away and I cannot breathe her in.

The space her leaving has created
I have attempted to fill
With bodies that numbed upon touching,
Among them I expected her opposite,
And found only forgeries.

Her wholeness I know to be a fiction of my making,
Still I cannot dismiss the longing for her;
It is a craving for sensation new flesh
Cannot wholly calm or cancel,
It is perhaps for more than her.

At night above the parks the stars are swarming.
The streets are thick with nostalgia;
I move through senseless routine and insensitive chatter
As if her going did not matter.
She is away and I cannot breathe her in.
I am ill simply through wanting her.

Seascape

Gulls kiss the sun
and you walk on the beach
afraid of the tide

from the sea's warm belly
a lobster crawls to
see if we've gone

but mouths still talk
and finding out my lips
I say to you

'stretch out your arms
like seaweed strangled by the wind'
you answer with silence

out of a seashell
a sandcrab pokes his head
and sniffs the salt wind

now afraid we sit in silence
and watching the sun go down
I ask you your name

Waves

And the one throwing the lifebelt,
Even he needs help at times,
Stranded on the beach,
Terrified of the waves.

In the Dying of Anything

Speaking only that our words might bend grasses,
make paths which are both simple and possible,
we talk together and failing with words we touch.
There is nothing simpler nor more human than this.

Once ignorant of any feeling's end
we dreamt in proportion to galaxies,
measuring each other against rainbows love burst,
fell softly soaking us.

But we lie quieter now,
older,
arms pressed out against darkness.
In the dying of anything walks a creature looking for its song:
huge, it bends down planets that it might ask them
the ways back to life again.

No longer one steady and running stream
we are glad to lie here,
catching what life and light we can.
There is nothing simpler, nothing more human than this.

Angel Wings

In the morning I opened the cupboard
and found inside it a pair of wings,
a pair of angel's wings.
I was not naïve enough to believe them real.
I wondered who had left them there.

I took them out the cupboard,
brought them over to the light by the window
and examined them.
You sat in the bed in the light by the window grinning.

'They are mine,' you said;
You said that when we met
you'd left them there.

I thought you were crazy.
Your joke embarrassed me.
Nowadays even the mention of the word angel
embarrasses me.

I looked to see how you'd stuck the wings together.
Looking for glue, I plucked out the feathers.
One by one I plucked them till the bed was littered.

'They are real,' you insisted,
your smile vanishing.

And on the pillow your face grew paler.
Your hands reached to stop me but
for some time now I have been embarrassed by the word
   angel.
For some time in polite or conservative company
I have checked myself from believing
anything so untouched and yet so touchable
had a chance of existing.

I plucked then
till your face grew even paler;
intent on proving them false
I plucked
and your body grew thinner.
I plucked till you all but vanished.

Soon beside me in the light,
beside the bed in which you were lying
was a mass of torn feathers;
glueless, unstitched, brilliant,
reminiscent of some vague disaster.

In the evening I go out alone now.
You say you can no longer join me.
You say
without wings it is not possible.
You say
ignorance has ruined us,
disbelief has slaughtered.

You stay at home
listening on the radio
to sad and peculiar music,
You who fed on belief,
who fed on the light I'd stolen.

Next morning when I opened the cupboard
out stepped a creature,
blank, dull, and too briefly sensual
it brushed out the feathers, gloating.
I must review my disbelief in angels.

Burning Genius

He fell in love with a lady violinist.
It was absurd the lengths he went to to win her affection.
He gave up his job in the Civil Service.
He followed her from concert hall to concert hall,
bought every available biography of Beethoven,
learnt German fluently,
brooded over the exact nature of inhuman suffering,
but all to no avail.

Day and night she sat in her attic room,
she sat playing day and night,
oblivious of him,
and of even the sparrows that perched on her skylight
    mistaking her music for food.

To impress her, he began to study music in earnest.
Soon he was dismissing Vivaldi and praising Wagner.
He wrote concertos in his spare time,
wrote operas about doomed astronauts and about monsters
    who,
when kissed,
became even more furious and ugly.
He wrote eight symphonies taking care to leave several
    unfinished,

It was exhausting.
And he found no time to return to that attic room.

In fact, he grew old and utterly famous.

And when asked to what he owed
his burning genius,
he shrugged and said little,

but his mind gaped back until he saw before him
the image of a tiny room,
and perched on the skylight the timid
skeletons of sparrows still listened on.

Somewhere Between Heaven and Woolworth's

She keeps kingfishers in their cages
And goldfish in their bowls,
She is lovely and is afraid
Of such things as growing cold.

She's had enough men to please her
Though they were more cruel than kind
And their love an act in isolation,
A form of pantomime.

She says she has forgotten
The feelings that she shared
At various all-night parties
Among the couples on the stairs,

For among the songs and dancing
She was once open wide,
A girl dressed in denim
With boys dressed in lies.

She's eating roses on toast with tulip butter,
Praying for her mirror to stay young;
On its no longer gilted surface
This message she has scrawled:

'O somewhere between Heaven and Woolworth's
I live I love I scold,
I keep kingfishers in their cages
And goldfish in their bowls.'

The Unicorn

She's pulled down the blinds now, she's locking the door,
a unicorn's just stepped down from the wall;
naked as snow on the eiderdown
it has rested its head and its horn.

She's pulled down the blinds now, it's warmer inside,
naked she crosses the room;
the eiderdown's blue and her hair is blonde
and white is the unicorn.

Dreaming, though both far from sleep,
both head and body spin around,
and humming deep into her veins
moves now the unicorn.

Frightened once by normal flesh
her body disallowed
ordinary shapes to entertain her,
even buried deep in dreams –

for touched too soon in hurrying rooms,
the walls, forests they became,
and into myth she faded,
leaf-eyed; birds sang inside her brain.

She's pulled down the blinds now, she's locked the door,
fists bunched tight against a wall;
the eiderdown's blue and her hair is blonde
and red now the unicorn.

Her Song

For no other reason than I love him wholly
I am here; for this one night at least
The world has shrunk to a boyish breast
On which my head, brilliant and exhausted, rests,
And can know of nothing more complete.

Let the dawn assemble all its guilts, its worries
And small doubts that, but for love, would infect
This perfect heart.
I am as far beyond doubt as the sun.
I am as far beyond doubt as is possible.

When into Sudden Beds

When through absence into sudden beds
You fall to ward
Off darkness and to share
For habit's sake some human warmth,

If who is now gone in dream returns
To ignite some loss and make
The hand that reaches seem
Blind, ignorant of your suffering,

Then, with a larger sympathy than once you owned,
Must you now turn, else all dark is yours
And beds, forever blind,
Will make within them wars.

Whatever's touched, shoulder, thigh or breast,
With some uncommon pain will burn
When for love you're asked to pay in kind,
And find you are not strong enough to turn.

Horror Story

At night someone drifts through these walls,
At night someone stands beside me saying
  Get up,
Get up from sleep, from the warm lull,
  Get up,
There is somewhere else to go.
Leave the womb behind you,
The womb in mint condition,
Leave it.
Leave it to its own fate,
Its prune fate.
  Get up.
The pillows smell of strangers;
All night the sheets howl.
  Get up
From the dead bed,
From the bed your mouth slaughtered.
You stink of nightmares,
  Get up,
There is somewhere else to go,
Somewhere not sucked dry,
Somewhere that does not terrify.
  Get up,
The heart has gone fat and blind.
While you slept
Paradise shrank to a single leaf.

Nightly and inevitably
I reach into the darkness to touch him,
And touching only my own flesh
I creep in terror from the bed's grave.

No doubt through these walls at night
Your own stranger drifts,
Invisible to me, mouthing the same message;
      Let's get up,
We have listened so often saying nothing
That we have become phantoms.

Rauin

A creature you will not bother to name
but that can name itself in anything,
I push up through the stems of flowers
and step out on to lawns.
I am a star-swan, am newly frozen rain
cracking under paws.
I am imagination; brushing against railings
they glow, I leave
light in trees, know not whether
it is a lawn or universe I am crossing.
So be quieter my friends, do not
talk too much of me;
some vision of this planet might come and go
while you put into words my wonder.
I am whatever wakes you from comfortable beds
to come shivering –
nightgowns around you –
to press faces against freezing cloud.
And I am what you step towards in wonder,
the rainbow found breathing in bushes,
the first creature seeing through mists
new planets floating.
I follow the ant in its tree-trunk world.
I am imagination,
when I enter your women they glow;
you would pull curtains back on them that heaven
might see its only rivals.

Are you watching me, here
with the lawns in your noses?
Whatever shape I take I will not
call you; I am silence,
in my immensity wander all your senses;
I am the paradise never lost only
you must evaporate before reaching me.

Park Note

Disgusted by the weight of his own sorrow.
I saw one evening
a stranger open wide his coat
and taking out from under it his heart
throw the thing away.

Away over the railings, out across the parks,
across the lakes and the grasses,
as if after much confusion
he had decided not to care but

to move on lightly, carelessly,
amazed and with a grin upon his face
that seemed to say, 'Absurd
how easily that was done.'

At Four O'Clock in the Morning

As all is temporary and is changeable,
So in this bed my love you lie,
Temporary beyond imagining;
Trusting and certain, in present time you rest,
A world completed.

Yet already are the windows freaked with dawn;
Shrill song reminds
Each of a separate knowledge;
Shrill light might make of love
A weight both false and monstrous.

So hush; enough words are used:
We know how blunt can grow such phrases as
Only children use without
Awareness of their human weight.

There is no need to impose upon feelings
Yesterday's echo.
I love you true enough;
Beyond this, nothing is expected.

Early in the Evening

I met her early in the evening
The cars were going home
I was twenty-four and dreaming
My head was full of shadows her brightness cancelled
Beneath her dress her breasts were pushing
It was early in the evening
Spring was only a few streets away
In the closed parks the leaves were trying
The pubs had nothing to give us
Early in the evening
When the street railings were burning
There was nothing much to do but to be together

She drifted into sleep early in the evening
Her head was on the pillow
The sun that fell about her
Drifted in the window
Early in the evening
Some birds still sang on rooftops
Their hearts could have fitted into egg-cups
It was early in the evening
The sky was going purple
Her dress lay on a chair by the window
Early in the evening she had shook it from her
She was awake and she was dreaming
Her head was free of shadows
Her belly was glowing

I had never imagined a body so loving
I had never imagined a body so golden
Early in the evening we had amazed one another
While the offices were closing
And couples grabbed at telephones
And all the lines were reaching
Early into evening
There was nothing much to do then
And nothing better either

Lethargy

You have dreamt so often of what you would do
If your life were irrevocably changed
That when you are forced finally from the route best
    understood
And on to another, less obvious way,
You think at first fantasy will sustain you.
Sink then dreamer into what might have been!
For though on the brilliant branch
The brilliant fruit still clings
It is no longer reached with ease,
And its dazzle's frightening.

One Another's Light

I do not know what brought me here
Away from where I've hardly ever been and now
Am never likely to go again.

Faces are lost, and places passed
At which I could have stopped,
And stopping, been glad enough.

Some faces left a mark,
And I on them might have wrought
Some kind of charm or spell
To make their futures work,

But it's hard to guess
How one person on another
Works an influence.
We pass, and lit briefly by one another's light
Hope the way we go is right.

Our Lives Had Grown So Empty

Remember the hibiscus we planted last spring?
Well, it flowered.
There is no other news.

No Taxis Available

It is absurd not knowing
where to go.

You wear the streets like an overcoat.
Certain houses are friends, certain houses
Can no longer be visited.
Old love-affairs lurk in doorways, behind windows
Women grow older. Neglection blossoms.

You have turned down numerous invitations,
Left the telephones unanswered, said 'No'
To the few that needed you.
Stranded on an island of your own invention
You have thrown out messages, longings.

How useless it is knowing that where you want to go
Is nowhere concrete.
The trains will not take you there,
The red buses glide past without stopping,

No taxis are available.

On a Horse Called Autumn

On a horse called Autumn
among certain decaying things
she rides inside me, and

no matter where I move
this woman's song
goes on ahead of me.

She sings of stables decaying
near where once
riders came,

and where now alone
her heart journeys, among
lies I made real.

Now riding in truth
what alterations can I make
knowing nothing will change?

Things stay the same:
Such journeys as hers
are the ones I care for.

Apart Together in Her Bed
We Lay

Apart together in her bed we lay
And of sharing a life we both despaired.
My excuse was the fear of being owned
And hers, though not the same,
We both knew was equally as lame.

The Heroine Bitches

I play my instrument, now like a lark,
perhaps like a nightingale, now perhaps
like the laughter of some girl
ready for anything.

I play, not so much to astonish, but to play.
Then what trickery is it,
what act of absurd fate
that the hero has chosen this moment to arrive?

He will try to overshadow me,
with his love-myth that blossoms on the hearts
of couples too dreamy to notice,
He will attempt to undermine me.

Surely outside the courts, surely in the streets among
the fair-grounds and markets,
among the drunken troubadours and sailors,
I would outshine him?

Heroes would look foolish there.
They belong adrift on oceans
where no one can contradict them and monsters
need not always happen.

What absurdity then that he comes
when I have least need of him?
With my playing I have caught
the attention of the whole crowd
and among them
several I've wanted.

Vanishing Trick

Your back is long and perfect, it is clear.
It moves away from me, it moves away, I watch it going.
In the morning I watch you gather up
longings mistakenly scattered.

I watch you gather up your face, your body,
watch till another creature walks about,
dressed and impatient.

You contained all there need be of love,
all there need be of jubilance and laughter you contained it.
And now you are its opposite.
You talk of going as if going were the smallest matter.

There do not have to be reasons for such changes,
there do not have to be.
In the morning bodies evaporate and nothing
can quite hold them together.

Suddenly everything changes.
Less than a second passes and nothing's the same.
Something that clung a moment ago lets go as if
all its clinging meant nothing.

Now in the bathroom the razors wait like a line of little
     friends,
they glow as much as roses,
they glow, glow with pain, with their own electricity,
they glow with darkness.

When you have gone they will turn their heads in my
     direction.
Inquisitive and eager they will welcome me,
but I will not listen.
I will try your vanishing trick and manage,
I will manage to feel nothing.

Towards Evening and Tired
   of the Place

Time to uproot again, there's much to be cancelled;
Your dreams, like useless trinkets, have come to nothing.
Across the harbour the lights have dullened,
In the town rain's scattered petals.
You are vague now about what things matter.
The years have ceased to preen themselves in front of mirrors.
The cafes do not always glitter, the women sit
Big-eyed and drained of laughter.
From their breasts you have detached your dreams,
They would have aged there.

You have shrugged off the moments in your life
When things have begun to matter,
Preferring to remain weightless,
Adrift in places where nothing has yet happened.
Believing there are better things than the best,
Brighter things than the brightest,
You have alighted like a butterfly on insubstantial flowers,
Have wasted your life in conversations with yourself,
Moved so long within your own shadow
That no weight can be felt, no commitments made.
Over all the world the rain falls like an answer.

A Few Questions about Romeo

And what if Romeo,
lying in that chapel in Verona,
miserable and spotty, at odds with everything,
what if he'd had a revelation from which
Juliet was absent?
What if, just before darkness settled
the arguments between most things,
through a gap in the walls he'd seen
a garden exploding,
and the pink shadow of blossom
shivering on stones?
What if,
unromantic as it seems,
her mouth, eyes, cheeks and breasts suddenly became
ornaments on a frame
common as any girl's?

Could he still have drunk that potion had he known
without her the world still glowed
and love was not confined
in one shape alone?

From the prison the weary imagine
all living things inhabit
how could either
not have wished to escape?
Poor Romeo, poor Juliet, poor human race!

The Wife

Absurdly, she thought Love was there for the taking,
Something gentle at her beck and call.
She thought it was her due, her given right;
That at her bidding Love would come submitting.
Then other needs took precedence,
For years she put all thought of it aside.
A dull husband, two kids, the house –
Like many others she made a compromise.
The slow drift to separate beds
Went by most unrecognized.
Then, long delayed by its other battles,
Unbidden and with a roaring arrogance Love came,
And she, caught up in its chaos and its flame,
Found her needs and Love's were not the same.

The Outgoing Song

On the warm grass enclosed now
by dull light and silence
your thoughts have fallen. Only

one bird that will insist on jabbering
breaks what calm
has come over you.

All worries, pains, all things that
you owned and were broken by
are reduced to this impassiveness.

For long now no one has brought
giant sorrows; small worries vanish,
spill out from you.

How quiet it is possible to grow!
Then why this want, this reaching out;
why the regrets then? The outgoing song?

News from the Gladland

Falling into the green and outstretched palm of the world
The messenger is visible and is heard to sing:

'Today I bring you good news, the same good news as ever:
Down by the wide lakes the giant suns have risen,
Lighting the sails of boats going outwards forever.

Today I bring you good news, the same good news as ever:
Autumn's sailors, disappearing over the rim of the world,
Are not lost nor drowned nor crying.
Their mouths are stuffed with apples.
Their bodies are cool as the morning's grasses.
Their lungs are opened up like flowers.

And today I bring you strange news, the same strange news as
    ever:
This country will never be lost,
Every morning it is born afresh,
Every morning it is born forever,
Yet the children who cross it laughing
(O strangest of mammals!)
Will not return if their sight is ruined.

And today I bring you good advice, simple advice the same as
    ever:
You must celebrate the morning in your blood,
For nothing dies there, nothing ends,
Over and over again you must invent yourselves,
True magicians, riding the senses of dust,
Know that with this gift you're blest.'

The Morning's Got a Sleepy Head

The morning's got a sleepy head;
it brings parcels of mist, dreams freshly woven,
bright mad gifts it's left on their pillows.

They move together, slower even
than the sun that above the wood's rising.
Learning not to hurry or bypass
the smallest of sensations,
they go to where lust and tenderness are words,
and words are meaningless.

They've reason for wanting to follow
each other out across the morning,
out to where the hazel opens
and the grass is softest flame.

Forever is one light behind them
that filled a summer,
spilt over into autumn with aches that dropped
when each had lost
the need to care quite hard enough.

Things go too quickly or else they dullen;
quick as the autumn marigold
skates the borders of whitening grass,
things go and nothing seems replaced.
The gap one makes in leaving is not filled.

The morning's got a sleepy head; it brings
parcels of mist, dreams freshly woven,
bright mad tears it's left on their pillows.

The Ice Maiden

Not out of snow or rain frozen,
not out of any of nature's gifts
I made an ice maiden

but it was the lonely freak
walking in my head
that first shaped and loved her.

And now later when cocksure it moves
through pubs through rooms
and stops to glance at her

it sees nothing clear. Only
those who surround her
it sees for what they are.

That she is as ordinary
as all I've touched
will not occur to me;

nor will the fact she needs
only a simple view of me.
I magnify her, make her

an excuse for the absence
of something deeper. Yet this
can hardly matter:

beyond what she is, all
is quite similar to her;
falls back into her.

You Come to Me Quiet as Rain Not Yet Fallen

You come to me quiet as rain not yet fallen
afraid of how you might fail yourself. Your
dress seven summers old is kept open
in memory of sex, smells warm, of boys,
and of the once long grass.
But we are colder now; we have not
love's first magic here. You come to me
quiet as bulbs not yet broken
out into sunlight.

The fear I see in your now lining face
changes to puzzlement when my hands reach
for you as branches reach. Your dress
does not fall easily, nor does your body
sing of its own accord. What love added to
a common shape no longer seems a miracle.
You come to me with your age wrapped in excuses
and afraid of its silence.

Into the paradise our younger lives made
of this bed and room
has leaked the world and all its questioning
and now those shapes terrify us most
that remind us of our own. Easier now
to check longings and sentiment,
to pretend not to care overmuch,
you look out across the years, and you come to me
quiet as the last of our senses closing.

The Tragedy

Behind the oven yesterday
I found a pencil-written note.
It had been there some years,
Brooding and awaiting its moment
Among the chip-fat and ketchup.

'Bastard,' it read,
'I'll not be back again.
It's after midnight. This time
I'm going forever.'

It was from someone whose name
I could not decipher.
Grease had obscured the signature.

I was not even sure whether
It was addressed to me.
Perhaps. Perhaps not.
I neither knew nor cared.

That is the tragedy.

The Cynic's Only Love Poem

Love comes and goes
And often it has paused,
Then come back to see
The damage it has caused.

You Missed the Sunflowers
at Their Height

You missed the sunflowers at their height,
Came back when they were bent and worn
And the gnats, half-froze, fell one by one
Into the last of the sprawling marigolds.

And as if linked to some spider thread
Made visible only because of rain,
You sat and watched the day come light
And hope leapt back into your brain,

And suddenly this surprising earth,
No longer clouded, was known again,
And all you had thought lost you found
Was simply for a time mislaid.

The Want

Where do longings go
When we let them go
And say we do not care?

They do not vanish into air,
But mingling with the blood
Create a poison there.

And where now the want,
The ache without a wound
That beat slow-time in the heart's
Once new-found core?

Relinquished,
Abandoned, all
That was raw!

Waiting

Be still world, be still tonight.
All about me seems frozen
In anticipation of her arrival.

The moth flattens its wings;
The blackbird's song is weighed down by rain.
The owl waits in a tunnel of leaves.

Be still world, be still tonight.
I am listening for the sound of her footsteps
Along a path muffled by shadows.

No matter that I know
This waiting is a sickness
I cannot stop waiting.

For too long she has been missing
From the night's vocabulary.
Be still world, be still in case she passes,

And once more the night roars with her absence.

Amour

She said I was a wolf in sheep's clothing.
Not true.
I was a lamb, in armour.

Probably It Is Too Early
in the Morning

Probably it is too early in the morning;
probably you have not yet risen
and the curtains float
like sails against the window.
But whatever, whatever the time, the place, the season,
here I am again at your door,
bringing a bunch of reasons why I should enter.

Probably it is too early inside you yet
for you to gather together what you are and speak;
but whatever, whatever the time, the place, the season,
it is certainly good to have come this far,
to know what I am and not mistrust.

The earth has many hands and doors upon
which these hands are knocking.
There are chairs for some on which to sit
more patient than the rest,
and here I am again, and again am knocking,
holding a fist of primonia,
dressed to kill,
clean dustless and idiotic.
I might be thought mad, insane or stupid;
my belief in you might be totally unfounded;
it might be called utterly romantic,

but what the hell?
Here I am again, and again am knocking.
But probably it is too early;
probably I'm too eager to come rushing towards you,
impatient to share what glows
while there is still
what glows around me.

I bang on the door of the world.
You are asleep behind it.
I bang on the door of the world
as on my own heart a world's been hammering.

Forgetmeknot

She loves him, she loves him not, she is confused:
She picks a fist of soaking grass and fingers it:
She loves him not.
The message passing from her head to heart
Has in her stomach stopped,
She cannot quite believe the information is correct:
She loves him not.
She knows her needs and yet
There is no special place where they can rest.
To be loved alone is not enough,
She feels something has been lost.
She picks a fist of soaking grass.
Her world is blank, she thinks perhaps it's meaningless.

Reading Between Graffiti

On a toilet wall the graffiti's bleak –
'FUCK A STRANGER TONIGHT'
Reads a message not there last week.
Other slogans, names and boasts
Seem jaded compared with this
Advice scrawled by Anonymous.
But the graffiti evokes an image of the crowd,
The lost, androgynous animal
That does not die but daily swells,
That longs for kindness then reveals
A different nature on toilet walls.
Yet let's give its authors credit enough
To understand how the night
Breeds in its drunken scribblers
Things wrongly written that are right.

Embroidered Butterflies

One afternoon you meet a young girl. She smiles at you,
It's summer and on the lakes the boats seem to burn.
She wears a dress through which you can see,
Half-hidden by embroidered butterflies,
Her breasts, small and perfect.

She is attentive; she is going nowhere and shows
How much she likes you.
Your routines fade again.
The hedges smell good and glitter.

She is easy to get on with. Not for a long time
Has someone opened with such obvious pleasure.
You are glad it is summer, and can lounge in parks
Or fall into rooms where she questions nothing.
For a moment she terrifies you with her freedom,
She's all over you laughing,
The dress she looked so good in earlier falls,
Unashamedly, like petals.

Then in the evening the butterflies are worn again.
You joke about them,
And when she laughs everything is changed –
She is young and then is not so young.
You understand her freedom, how (like the butterflies)
It belongs to certain seasons, certain weathers.
You are obsessed.

You ask her to stay, but it's evening and she says
'It's not possible.' For one day only on your life
Was this butterfly embroidered.

Near the Factory Where They Make the Lilac Perfume

Near the factory where they make the lilac perfume
is a cemetery where those who have abandoned their dead
are long gone with them.
Decades of weeds have glued the broken slabs together.
Ice-numb, a song-thrush hops about as if
to locate a particular name.
A few stones stand out,
as white and tidy as the suburb that bred you.

A January afternoon. The sky's the colour of bone,
and all the epitaphs to do with love
have sunk back into ageing stone.
Wishing to believe this factory's manufactured lie,
one that makes women's flesh and their graves
smell sweeter,
I close my eyes and let the day's trash leak from me.
Helped by the scent of lilac-blossom and rain
memory hauls you back again.

January Gladsong

Seeing as yet nothing is really well enough arranged
the dragonfly will not yet sing
nor will the guests ever arrive
quite as naked as the tulips intended.
Still, because once again I am wholly glad of living,
I will make all that is possible step out of time
to a land of giant hurrays! where the happy monsters dance
and stomp darkness down.

Because joy and sorrow must finally unite and the small heart-
beat of sparrow be heard above jet-roar, I will sing
not of tomorrow's impossible paradise
but of what now radiates.
Forever the wind is blowing the white clouds in someone's
    pure direction.

In all our time birdsong has teemed and couples known
that darkness is not forever.
In the glad boat we sail the gentle and invisible ocean
where none have ever really drowned.

A Drop of Unclouded Blood

All day I will think of these cities floating fragile
across the earth's crust
and of how they are in need
of a drop of magic blood
a drop of unclouded blood

All day I will think of snow and the small
violets like a giant's blood
splashed at random on the earth
All day I will stroll about hoping
for a drop of unclouded blood
to fall into my veins

I need my body to move loose through the world
Need my fingers to touch the skin
of children adrift in their temporary world
Beneath their dreaming is a drop of blood
refusing the sun's heat
a drop of blood more pure than any other blood

I need to walk through the pale light
that occupies the world
and believe it when a drop of blood says
Listen,
paradise is never far away
and simpler than you think it

I need to sever all connection with the habits
that make the heart
love only certain things
I need a drop of magic blood for that
a drop of unclouded blood

You Have Gone to Sleep

The nerves tense up and then:
You have gone to sleep.
Something not anchored in love drifts out of reach.
You have gone to sleep, or feign sleep,
It does not matter which.
Into the voice leaks bitterness.
The throat dries up, the tongue
Swells with complaints.
Once sleep was simply sleep.
The future stretched no further than
The pillow upon which your head was resting.
There were no awkward questions in the world,
No doubts caused love to fade
To a numbed kiss or howl,
Or caused trust to vanish.
You have gone to sleep.
A moment ago I found
Your mouth on mine was counterfeit.
Your sleep is full of exhaustions,
I cannot calm you,
There is no potion to wake you.
Do what I will, say what I will,
It is a sleep from which I am exiled.
You have gone to sleep,
A planet drifts out of reach.
If I spoke all night it would be no use,
You would not wake,

And silence, like words, you would no doubt
Mistake for ignorance.
So sleep. Across our window's small patch of Heaven
The stars like sheep are herded,
And, like a satellite, objective time
Circles calendars and mocks
The wounds we think are huge.
Sleep, don't be so tense.
There is no longer a need of barriers,
No need of dumb defence.
You are understood.
This night is the last on which there will be
Any kind of pretence.
Tomorrow something else might wake
What's gone to sleep.

A Valentine

To be with one another forever and to have no doubt
(Nor feel exhaustion at the prospect)
Is the goal of those who, like us,
Speak in whispers through the night,
Whose one fear is of how Eternity just might
Be too short a time,
And for whom the briefest separation is a crime.

Because There Were
No Revelations at Hand

Because there were no revelations at hand
And the day being dark
The numerous prophets were elsewhere biding their time,
I went down to some pool's edge
Where various streams were mixing
And met there a bird with a mouthful of songs.

It fed them to a fish the pool contained;
To the grass also, and then to the trees
It fed its songs.

I wanted to go back and tell them all
Of what had been found.
But the day was dark,
And because no revelations were supposed to be at hand
I stayed there alone.

And standing on the luminous grass
Though there was no prayer in my brain
I spoke with the fish then and found
The lack of anything revealed to be
A revelation of a kind.

End of Story

She talked about so much –
About the blank nights that had nagged away at her,
About the husband long gone, the children settled.
She talked about the empathy of inanimate things,
About the moon's trick of whistling after the tides to call them
    back,
She talked about acquisitions as old as dust.
But she would not talk about the present,
About the things that mattered, about the things she said
    bored her.
We sat in a hillside garden before dawn, huddled in our
    overcoats.
The brazier between us glowed like a glass of magma.
She talked on and on – about the forthcoming snow,
About how once as a child she had seen icicles
Hanging from a tree's black branches.
Her words tumbled out, tumbled and fell over each other,
Her sentences indecipherable confessions,
Laments strangled at birth.
She spoke of everything but of what she wanted to speak
And so nothing was said,
No matter that the time for going was upon us
Still nothing was said.
The wind tasted of raspberries.
Dark green rain collected in the roots of the pine trees.
Down in the harbour a boat was unloading its cargo.
As the darkness leaked away we stood to leave,

But not even then did the silence behind her words
   take precedence,
Not even then.
We went down the hillside path together,
Passed the dead cafes, the blinking neon, the nets,
The coils of rope, the yawning dogs, the sleeping shadows.
And then she went one way, and I another.

The Likelihood

At some time or other the dust will change its mind.
It will cease to be dust.
It will start over again.
It will reconstitute itself,
become skin,
become a fingernail or perhaps
a heart beating slowly.
Whatever, let's keep our eyes open
in case we miss the moment
of the dust's rebellion,
and our ears open
for the small whisper of
'I'm fed up being dust,' or
'I long to be an apple polished
against the sleeve
of a child I'd forgotten!'
It might be the dust buried beneath frost speaking,
or the dust of old machinery,
or the melancholic dust of friends
who believed in dying.
It might even be the dust of the moths
God left uninvented.
Against a pile of such dust I have weighed
the likelihood of you returning.

Inessential Things

What do cats remember of days?

They remember the ways in from the cold,
the warmest spot, the place of food.
They remember the places of pain, their enemies,
the irritation of birds, the warm fumes of the soil,
the usefulness of dust.
They remember the creak of a bed, the sound
of their owner's footsteps,
the taste of fish, the loveliness of cream.
Cats remember what is essential of days.
Letting all other memories go as of no worth
they sleep sounder than we,
whose hearts break remembering so many
inessential things.

The Recognition

In your late sixties now, perhaps older,
Likely to be alive somewhere, looking in mirrors still,
Or dead, with all things accounted for and put aside.
Decades have passed since I last thought about you
Yet it is only tonight that, finally, I understand you,
Realize how you must have felt
Lying beside me in that long-gone room
Listening to the bark of a dog or the rattle of freight
On the world's muted periphery.
You were twice my age then,
And half a lifetime beyond my reach;
Such a weight of knowledge separated flesh from flesh
And amongst all that was mutual
Nothing could be equal.
Only tonight do I recognize the bleakness,
The sadness that overwhelmed you
And sent you hurrying back
To the safe harbour of your peers.
It invades me now as I stare at this girl,
So new and vulnerable beside me
And wonder if, half a lifetime hence,
She too might think such thoughts about me.

I Caught a Train that Passed the Town Where You Lived

I caught a train that passed the town where you lived.
On the journey I thought of you.
One evening when the park was soaking
You hid beneath trees, and all round you dimmed itself
As if the earth were lit by gaslight.
We had faith that love would last forever.

I caught a train that passed the town where you lived.

The Bee's Last Journey
to the Rose

I came first through the warm grass
Humming with Spring,
And now swim through the evening's
Soft sunlight gone cold.
I'm old in this green ocean,
Going a final time to the rose.

North wind, until I reach it
Keep your icy breath away
That changes pollen into dust.
Let me be drunk on this scent a final time,
Then blow if you must.

Letting Go

The goal's simple enough,
But so much harder to attain
Than at first we imagined:

We want to jettison the past,
Let go what we do not need
But cannot part with.

For the past howls,
Claws at the soul,
Frightened of leaving.

It clings to us,
One more addiction
To add to the rest.

Hoping to let go,
How complicated such
Simple longings grow.

I Tried to Find My Voice

I tried to find my voice, a voice lost
In a night thickened by paranoia,
In a night crowded out by doubts
It could not articulate.
I had let go of it through negligence,
As at a carnival one lets go a child's hand.

I rummaged through a jumble sale of bodies,
Listened to advice devoid of meaning;
My voice was like a moth, its few colours
Worn to exhaustion.
It was drunk and lost, it was battered
And flung everywhere.

I tried to find it in the beds
Of solemn girls disguised as women,
I tried to find it among the men I envied.
I searched for it among its own inventions.

I had arranged my life around that voice.
Absurdly relied on it to explain
Who and what I was, as if either mattered.
In strange towns I used it to advantage.
Whatever it could fish out from the night I accepted.

No matter; it was the one voice I let delude me.
Maybe it was getting the better of me,
Maybe it was envious and screamed at times,
Certainly it said things of which I'd grown ashamed,
But I forgave it its blindness and tantrums
Hoping it would change.

And now it is beyond change.
My mouth cannot find it.
I have lost it; and no longer wish it back.
In winter I will make a voice out of snow,
In spring I will make a voice out of flowers,
In summer and autumn I will make a voice
With what is at hand.

The complaints it carried like credentials are misplaced
And its mouthful of reasons are blown away,
And its mouthful of tragedies
Have become light as dandelion seeds.

And Heart is Daft

Without understanding any pain but that
which inside her anyway is made,
this creature singled out creates
havoc with intelligence. And heart is daft,
is some crazy bird let loose and blind
that slaps against the night and has
never anywhere to go. And when a tongue's
about to speak some nonsense like
'Love is weak, or blind, or both', then comes
this crazy bird, pecks at it like a worm.

If Words Were More Her Medium than Touch

She might have said, if words
Were more her medium than touch:
'Near you is one
Frighteningly real who cannot plan;
Whose heart's a cat from which
Your habits dart like birds;
Who had no weight until you gave
False lust and words like "lost"
A chance to twist
My body into complicated shapes.'

Her Advice

She said, 'Come from the window,
Dreamer, do not drift too far from me;
In other rooms the party's growing old.
Leave off star-gazing for a time,
Leave Heaven to dance alone.
Come from the window;
Dreamer, unlike myself,
Heaven left alone will not grow bored.
The wonder you seek there
You yourself when younger formed.'
And she was right.
Though our longings do not end with what she says,
She was right. Without her help
Night would have been simply night,
The stars of little consequence, and not very bright.

Bare Necessity

Now that I am free
Of all that might be said
To keep and entrap me,
How much deeper the need
To keep her beside me.

When romance flakes away
And infatuation vanishes
How clearly I see her.
From beneath all I have superimposed upon her
The skeleton rises.

Love, how stark the light needed
To see through your disguises,
To see through to where
One can begin to find her.

Sometimes it Happens

And sometimes it happens that you are friends and then
You are not friends,
And friendship has passed.
And whole days are lost and among them
A fountain empties itself.

And sometimes it happens that you are loved and then
You are not loved,
And love is past.
And whole days are lost and among them
A fountain empties itself into the grass.

And sometimes you want to speak to her and then
You do not want to speak,
Then the opportunity has passed.
Your dreams flare up, they suddenly vanish.

And also it happens that there is nowhere to go and then
There is somewhere to go,
Then you have bypassed.
And the years flare up and are gone,
Quicker than a minute.

So you have nothing.
You wonder if these things matter and then
As soon as you begin to wonder if these things matter
That's when they begin to cease to matter,
And caring is past.
And a fountain empties itself into the grass.

Meeting Again

Tell me, I asked,
What became of that fantastic dress
That flowed over you as if made of water?

Put aside now.
God knows at the back of what cupboard it's hung.
I forgot it years ago.

But not I.
And tell me, that necklace the colour of a summer's sky,
So blue at your throat it astonished.
What became of it?

In some box of junk now.
Those stones were baubles,
Nothing else.
I forgot them years ago.

But not I.
And tell me, what became of the boys you adored
In the days when safety-nets were made of love alone?

Gone into oblivion now.
I see no sense in looking back.
I have buried their memory under regrets as heavy as stones.

But not I.
For me that dress still flows,
Those baubles
Are still the colour of the sky.

Oh yes? she said,
But not for I.

The Understudies

Middle aged, I sit in the corner of a public bar.
As undesired by me as I by them
I view those young girls as if from afar,
Replicas of women loved long ago.
Then one walks in – entirely new –
And catching a familiar scent rising from her hair
I am blown away by ripe despair,
And am reminded yet again of how the years pass,
And of how all our pleasures are as brief
As morning frost upon the glass.

Yes

Last night I dreamt again of Adam returning
To the Garden's scented, bubbling cauldron.

Eve was beside him,
Their shadows were cut adrift
And the hum of bees was in their blood,

And the world was slow and good and all
The warm and yawning newness of their flesh
Was fixed forever in the glow of 'Yes'.

So Late in the Evening

As she goes home this evening
Her head and body still full of him
What can she say
To the one who waits impatient
Waits in a room rehearsing
A list of stale arguments
Adding up and subtracting
Like a sickly accountant
A registry of hurts?
What reasons can be given
What excuses can be made
So late in the evening,
So very late in the evening
As she wanders home
Her head and body singing
Singing and knowing
No reasons are needed?
For she wears her joy
As a kind of armour,
And all her excuses are vanishing
And all her guilt is melting

And she is careless finally
And is finally loving,
And she is wrapped in the scent of the one
From whom she is walking,
As evidence for the one
To whom she is going
For a final time
So late in the evening.

Autumn Joke

I thought it was you hurrying behind me,
About to say, 'Stop, nothing's changed!'
But it was only an old sycamore leaf
Blown by the wind, the joker.

Wound Cream

Perhaps it is the way Love's promoted;
You'd think it came in a jar,
Something that could be spread
Over all that bothers us,
A heal-all, a wound cream,
A media promoted fairy-tale
Gutted of darkness.

Though its contradictions
Nail us to each other
And the hunger for it
Can be our undoing,
We still use it as a prop,
As proof we are living.

How hard to do other than
Give it precedence, forgetting
How friendship outlives it,
Commits fewer crimes,
Wears its name at times.

When You Wake Tomorrow

I will give you a poem when you wake tomorrow.
It will be a peaceful poem.
It won't make you sad.
It won't make you miserable.
It will simply be a poem to give you
when you wake tomorrow.

It was not written by myself alone.
I cannot lay claim to it.
I found it in your body.
In your smile I found it.
Will you recognize it?

You will find it under your pillow.
When you open the cupboard it will be there.
You will blink in astonishment,
shout out, 'How it trembles!
Its nakedness is startling! How fresh it tastes!'

We will have it for breakfast –
on a table lit by loving,
at a place reserved for wonder.
We will give the world a kissing open
when we wake tomorrow.

We will offer it to the sad landlord out on the balcony,
to the dreamers at the window.
To the hand waving for no particular reason
we will offer it.
An amazing and most remarkable thing,
we will offer it to the whole human race
which walks in us
when we wake tomorrow.

The Stolen Orange

When I went out I stole an orange
I kept it in my pocket
It felt like a warm planet

Everywhere I went smelt of oranges
Whenever I got into an awkward situation
I'd take the orange out and smell it

And immediately on even dead branches I saw
The lovely and fierce orange blossom
That smells so much of joy

When I went out I stole an orange
It was a safeguard against imagining
There was nothing bright or special in the world

Hesitant

He sees beyond her face another face.
It is the one he wants.
He stares at it in amazement;
There is nothing anywhere quite like it.
There is nothing else that's wanted.

She sees beyond his face another face.
It stares at her in amazement.
She stares back, equally amazed.
Just why, she can't quite answer.
She simply wants it.

These faces have been waiting now
A long time to be introduced.
If only the faces in front of the faces
Would do something about it.

Dear Thief

You dress in silence
And tiptoe down the stairs
Never to return to this bed,
Still hot with longings.
It's six in the morning.
The bed creaks and clinks
Like an oven cooling.

Dear thief, I wonder if you realize
What it is you have stolen?

I Have Changed the Numbers
on My Watch

I have changed the numbers on my watch,
and now perhaps something else will change.
Now perhaps
at precisely 6 a.m.
you will not get up
and gathering your things together
go forever.
Perhaps now you will find it is
far too early to go,
or far too late,
and stay forever.

An Obsession

There are so many well-rehearsed farewells that have gone
   unsaid,
So many partings planned in the mind that the heart
Has not had the courage to follow through,
Although it knows, clairvoyant that it is,
The future holds no trace of you.
First it was your intelligence I loved,
Desire followed.
Your mouth blew the monotony of years aside.
I loved you first without expectation,
But then buckled under the weight
Of absurd hope. I loved you with a passion that lost its way
And became a sickness. Such was my obsession
I mistook your fear for coolness, forgetting
How this late on there are no new beginnings without betrayal.
I loved the tiredness of your breasts,
The softness of your stomach;
I was overawed by how all your adult life
Blood and milk have flowed endlessly from you.
You became my addiction, an obsession
Cured only by withdrawal.
Whenever I tried to break free of you
Timid reason was unravelled by love.

So many partings in the mind the heart
Has not had the courage to follow through.
God knows I tried, but in the darkness in which
Your body was another darkness,
Your mouth expertly stopped my questions,
Sabotaged the night's small vocabulary,
Sought to avoid all further duplicity.

You Go into Town

When she has gone you go into town.
You have learnt the places where the lonely go,
You know their habits, their acts of indifference
      practised so efficiently.
You have learnt how those who are hardly children
Can be most open, how the most obviously sensual
Tire you with questions; you have learnt.
How inside them all
Terror is waiting.

At certain times the galleries close; in certain areas
      the supermarkets fill with strangers.
At certain times the bars swell with gossip,
      then people tire and look around.
Like one from another place and time
You've stepped through this ritual knowing
How on each face the promises are hollow,
How scarce any spontaneous greetings.

When she has gone you go into town.
But in no other face can you trace her,
In other bodies can be found only
      an echo of her.
    You know the places where the lonely go,
You know their habits, their acts of indifference
      practised so efficiently.

Whose Body Has Opened

Whose body has opened
Night after night
Harbouring loneliness,
Cancelling the doubts
Of which I am made,
Night after night
Taste me upon you.

Night and then again night,
And in your movements
The bed's shape is forgotten.
Sinking through it I follow,
Adrift on the taste of you.

I cannot speak clearly about you.
Night and then again night,
And after a night beside you
Night without you is barren.

I have never discovered
What alchemy makes
Your flesh different from the rest,
Nor why all that's commonplace
Comes to seem unique,

And though down my spine one answer leaks
It has no way to explain itself.

Her Coldness Explained

She said no man had ever hurt her,
She, who beside me like a statue lay.
And she would have me believe her heart
Was cold, and like a statue made of clay.

What? What did she say?
No man had ever hurt her?
She is so wrong.
Through her dreams her father walks night-long.

Road Song

This evening at least I do not care
where the journey will be ending;
only a landscape softened now
by song and slow rainfall fills me.

The rest of things, her body crushed
against the whitest pillows, regrets
and the more concrete failures
are exiled and done with.

There is nowhere specially to get to.
The towns are identical, each one passed
takes deeper into evening
what sorrows I've brought with me.

In my head some voice is singing
a song that once linked us;
it has ceased to be of importance;
another song might replace it.

Now only my gawky shadow occupies
these roads going nowhere,
that by small towns are linked
and that by the darkness are cancelled.

The Word

I did not know the workings of her mind;
Only that, from time to time in sleep,
She would let slip a single word,
One that, if heard, might have unlocked
Part of her awkwardness,
Her holding back.

She would curl up beside me in the bed
And I would strain to catch that word she said,
Though hearing it was something I had begun to dread.
It was mumbled; full of distress.
Muted by the thickness of her sleep,
How could a single word make her weep?

Too often and too obsessively I asked, but she
Was unable to explain what tormented her and I
Was unable to admit as to why
I wished so much to know,
And would not let my inquisition go.
Long after she had gone the mystery of that word lived on,

And it's only lately that I have come to understand
Why I could not hear what it was she said:
I did not listen for her sake, but for my own.
I did not listen out of love,
But out of fear –
And that alone is why I could not hear.

And now perhaps elsewhere, in her own or in another's bed
Someone with wiser ears than mine
Will have understood what it was she said,
And perhaps because of this
She will have let that word go.

It is something I will never know.

Tristan, Waking in His Wood, Panics

Do not let me win again, not this time,
Not again. I've won too often and know
What winning is about. I do not want to possess;
I do not want to. I will not want you.

Every time a thing is won,
Every time a thing is owned,
Every time a thing is possessed,
It vanishes.

Only the need is perfect, only the wanting.
Tranquillity does not suit me;
I itch for disasters.

I know the seasons; I'm familiar with
Those things that come and go,
Destroy, build up, burn and freeze me.

I'm familiar with opposites
And taste what I can,
But still I stay starving.

It would be easy to blame an age,
Blame fashions that infiltrate and cause
What was thought constant to change.

But what future if I admitted to no dream beyond the one
From which I'm just woken?
Already in the wood the light grass has darkened.

Like a necklace of deaths the flowers hug the ground;
Their scents, once magically known,
Seem now irretrievable.

Survivor

Coming out of the storm the butterfly surprised us,
A survivor, alighting on a snapped branch,
Its wings still with their blue, crocus-coloured dust;
If only we'd had its luck
Coming out of our own storm, flightless now.

Sleepy

Sleepy, you had nothing to tell me.
Yet in such moments was no song nor sound
Nor laugh nor anything so pure
As the silence with which you presented me.
Spilt over into oblivion and then spilt back again,
You came back speechless.
O planet face! I still smell the forest in your neck!
Still taste the stream in your mouth!
And your kiss that dropped on to my skin like rain
Still shivers there!

Don't Ask

Tell me, love, what were you thinking of?

I was thinking how there are certain times of the night
when the dead wipe the frost from their souls and weep.

Of nothing simpler?

Of a courtyard I once visited, and of a woman
standing beside a statue covered in snow.

Of no one else? No one nearer?

She was so beautiful,
had she been made of nettles I'd have wanted her.

Why think of her now, at this moment?

Because I am still mixing the ashes of the dead and of dead
    obsessions.

Why answer me like this?

Because I am bankrupt of small comforts, of small deceits.
Because we two are new, and without history,
and treasonous memory sleeps in so many beds.

Over All We Are a Shadow Falls

It's hardly dawn but still we feel
Exhausted by what's left undone.
Over all we are a shadow falls.

The gifts we put aside
When we reach for them again are gone.
Over all we are a shadow falls.

Did we believe better things would replace
The things we let go? I think that's so.
Over all we are a shadow falls.

Each night in the vastness of our bed
We planned a future that by the light was dead.
Over all we are a shadow falls.

Our souls grow smaller with each dream deferred.
Now a different kind of night comes on.
Blink, and one or other of us will be gone.
Over all we are a shadow falls.

The Shadow-Puppet's Lament

Not quite drunk yet, I lean across the table
And gossip with my shadow.
We have intimate conversations
About the day's non-events,
About where they are leading and
The brightness they have fled from.
It smiles at my attempts to give substance
To that skeleton, Memory.

My shadow munches on the shadow of an apple,
And does not fill me.

I listen in horror as it complains
Of the raw edge gone from love,
And though I wish to fault all it says
My arguments are insubstantial.
It has an army of confederates to back
Every claim it can make against me.

Like a shabby magician
It conjures up the past,
Parades before me
All my mistakes,
My indiscretions.
It has drawn into itself
Everything for which I hungered.

Even in darkness I cannot escape it:
At night I dream of a stream that flows
Undauntingly through all things,
That clears away longings so old
They have festered.
My shadow sits beside it, thirsting.

Recently an avalanche of deaths
Has softened its tongue.
It asks questions of me
So simple they can hardly be answered.
When did you last weep?
Was there a witness?

It has begun to speak of what is still felt
For a woman not seen these last few years.
It can no longer remember which of us
Loved her best,
Nor even if that love was real,
Or a shadow.

I remember once how after she had gone
I sat like this in a different room.
I think it was only my shadow that wept,
And went out into the night in search of her.

They've Heard about You

A thousand questions filled my ears.
They were from friends, all asking about you,
All curious, all besotted, and all already
Courting chaos.

Those questions sizzled like fireworks,
Each one was full of golden sparks,
Each one buzzed with hunger.
Each one was too dangerous to answer.

See what you do to people?
If I could bottle and sell you in the markets
The world would be on fire.

April Morning Walk

So many of those girls I longed for are gone now,
Gone to ash that skin so inexpertly kissed,
Those stomachs I was hot for, gone beyond diaries into flames.
When the years tore up their surface beauty and threw it away
Like the bright wrappings on a parcel
What was left was what links all the breathing world, an
    empathy,
The buried knowledge of our going.
It's so easy to forget how the years have poured away
And taken out of sequence and before their time
So many who deserved longer on this lush earth.

Along the streets in which I walked with them
The horse chestnut leaves are opening like Chinese fans.
The dawn's clear light varnishes houses and gardens
And freezes forever under its glittering surface
So much half-remembered anguish.

Fingers Have Bruised Your Skin
the Way a Fallen Peach is Bruised

You arrive at the party late,
Though awake, your mouth still looks asleep,
A half-open trap, swollen and relaxed.
One look from you turns me inside out –
I can only guess
Whose fingers beneath that dress
Have bruised your skin the way
A fallen peach is bruised.
You walk up close.
The scent of you evokes a bed's oasis.

Poem Written in the Street
on a Rainy Evening

Everything I lost was found again.
I tasted wine in my mouth.
My heart was like a firefly; it moved
Through the darkest objects laughing.

There were enough reasons why this was happening
But I never stopped to think about them.
I could have said it was your face,
Could have said I'd drunk something idiotic,

But no one reason was sufficient,
No one reason was relevant.
My joy outshone dull surroundings.

A feast was spread; a world
Was suddenly made edible.
And there was forever to taste it.

That Dress, This Shirt

That dress won't stop you growing older, no matter how you
    wear it –
Nor will this baggy shirt I wear disguise any more
A stomach growing fatter by the hour.
Now that we no longer have Time's currency to squander,
Let's get used to the raw material we are,
Let's celebrate this far harder adventure
And stop carrying about the dead weight of Ago.
That dress, this shirt; we place them over chairs in rooms
Beside beds that set sail each night without expectation,
With us the crew, held together by love and by the faith
That we are buoyant enough to see any darkness through.

These Boys Have Never
Really Grown into Men

These boys have never really grown into men,
despite their disguises, despite their adult ways,
their sophistication, the camouflage of their kindly smiles.
They are still up to their old tricks,
still at the wing-plucking stage. Only now
their prey answers to women's names.
And the girls, likewise, despite their disguises,
despite their adult ways, their camouflage of need,
still twist love till its failure seems not of their making;
something grotesque migrates hourly
between our different needs,
and is in us all like a poison.
How strange I've not understood so clearly before
how liars and misers, the cruel and the arrogant
lie down and make love like all others,
how nothing is ever as expected, nothing is ever as stated.
Behind doors and windows nothing is ever as wanted.
The good have no monopoly on love.
All drink from it. All wear its absence like a shroud.

A Few Sentences about Beauty

When something vanished from her face,
When something banished its first light
It left a puzzle there,
And I wanted to go to her and say,
'It is all imagining and will change,'
But that would have been too much a lie,
For beauty does reach some kind of height,
And those who hunger for her now
Tomorrow might
Have a less keen appetite.
Yet beauty sinks deeper than the flesh,
And men seeking only surfaces
Will never know
What it is they have let go.

Her Ghost

What was it about her that without her
The world grew dull?

The memory of her nakedness –
How lovely she was and free-spirited
Is imprinted on me still

Though gone
I cannot get her voice out of my ears
I cannot wipe her smile from my retina

Friends say it's like any bereavement –
That she will haunt me less and less
But though some ghosts are like thistledown,
Blown away by time

If they had known her they would have understood
Other ghosts are immortal

What was it about her that without her
The world grew dull?

As sunlight burnt off frost
So she burnt off the ice I wore like armour.

Love Poem in February

Snow in the valley, snow
Filling the world's mouth

And the river flows under a cataract of frost

Elsewhere a pool looks up at the moon,
Blinks when a cloud passes over

Bleak memory trudges down a road
In search of – of what?

Of a time before her?

Silence.
An owl's hoot is frozen to its beak.

The falling snow white-washes all betrayals.

INDEX OF FIRST LINES